5-minute
Diwali
Stories for Kids

Introduction

Diwali has a profound spiritual significance like every other Indian festival. It is celebrated yearly in the Kartik month on Amavasya (new moon day), the darkest night of the month. Therefore, the majority of celebration revolves around light and how it has the strength to illuminate even the darkest of nights. In many sections of Hinduism, Diwali also marks the Hindu New Year and is celebrated with a lot of joy. This 2,500-year-old festival symbolizes purity, love, goodness, and wisdom.

Although the festival of Diwali brings every part of the world under one roof of goodness, love, and light, different folks and communities believe it to have originated from different roots. All the folktales of origin of Diwali are fascinating.

In this book, you will find 12 different stories, which will get you in the mood for celebration. The first 6 stories are adaptations of the most popular folktales related to Diwali. Your child will get to know Hindu deities and their story.

In the second part, you will find another 6 stories describing Diwali preparations and celebrations. That helps you to feel the atmosphere of the festival and immerse your kid in the atmosphere of celebration.

Every story is to be read in 5-minutes. They are the best to read in the meantime or at bedtime. We hope the book will help your kid understand and feel the atmosphere of Diwali and teach about Indian culture.

Contents

Diwali
Myths & Legends

The Return of Lord Rama and His Wife Sita

Once upon a time there lived Lord Rama, the brave prince of Ayodhya. He had a jealous stepmother Kaikeyi who didn't want Rama to rule the kingdom. King Dashrath, Lord Rama's father loved his son dearly but had to fulfill queen Kaikeyi's wish. He banished Lord Rama to the forest for 14 years with his wife Devi Sita. Prince Lakshmana, his younger brother accompanied them too.

On listening to this news, the people of Ayodhya were very sad. They shed tears and paid respects to the trio.

In the forest, Lord Rama, Sita, and Lakshmana started living a simple life. They lived and worked in the forest, away from the comforts of a palace.

One day Ravana, the demon king of Lanka (now Srilanka) heard of the beauty of Lord Rama's wife, Devi Sita from his sister. Ravana was a famous scholar, having studied all four religious scriptures (Vedas). But his knowledge made him arrogant and greedy. He decided to find Sita and started his journey. He traveled a long time and finally, found Sita. She was so beautiful that he wanted to marry her despite the fact she was Lord Rama's wife.

Ravana sent a golden deer to distract Rama and then Lakshmana away from Sita. He changed his form to that of an old sage (Rishi) and asked Sita for alms. Sita did not want to disrespect a sage by rejecting to give him her help. So to give alms, when Sita stepped out, Ravana kidnapped her and took her to Lanka.

In Lanka, Ravana tried to convince Sita to marry him but Sita never accepted him. Due to a curse, Ravana couldn't force her and thus had to keep waiting for Sita to change her mind.

Rama and Lakshmana were very unhappy and sad to find Sita missing. They searched for her in every corner of the forest. Lord Hanuman, the monkey god of the epic was a devout follower of Lord Rama. So, he decided to help the brothers. He flew into the sky and started searching for Sita. He finally found her and informed Lord Rama about her sad state.

Lord Rama said, "We need to talk to Ravana and tell him this is wrong. He cannot keep Sita there against her wish!"

But Lord Rama couldn't fly. Hanuman stepped forward and said, "Oh my Lord, I can fly and I can reach Lanka without any problem. Allow me to be your messenger."

Lord Rama and Lakshmana both agreed that this will be a good idea and Hanuman flew to Lanka. He reached Ravana's palace and told,
"O king of demons, I am here as a messenger of Lord Rama. You cannot trap Mother Sita against her wishes. Release her!"

Ravana laughed in arrogance.

"Go tell that Rama of yours to come here and fight me if he wants his wife back. And you! You will get the punishment for ordering the king of Lanka!" He ordered his soldiers to burn Hanuman's tail. But Hanuman being a god, grew his tail to enormous length and flew away from Lanka without being harmed.

Hanuman hurried back to the brothers and explained everything to them. On listening to Hanuman, Rama and his brother were enraged and decided to wage a war to rescue Sita. They started talking to and assembling people for the war. With the help of monkeys called vanaras and no help from the kingdom Ayodhya, the brothers traveled toward Lanka.

The Indian Ocean between India and Lanka made it difficult for Lord Rama's army to reach the other shore. Then the monkey called Nala came forward to build a bridge between two islands. The vanaras completed the architecture of the 80-mile-bridge using nothing but rocks in just 5 days.

The army of vanaras along with the princes of Ayodhya defeated all the demon-warriors one by one, ending the list with Ravana. Only one demon, Vibhishana, one of Ravana's brothers was saved because he took shelter on Lord Rama's side.

At the end of the war, Sita was finally reunited with Rama. On their reunion, many gods showered flowers from the sky. The couple cried tears of happiness. Also, the 14 years that they had to live in the forest away from their kingdom happily ended. The trio, along with their devout follower Hanuman, return to Ayodhya.

The day they returned to Ayodhya was the new moon day. The sky was dark but the overjoyed people of Ayodhya decorated the entire city with earthen lamps (diyas) and lit up the night. They sang songs of praise and shared sweets to celebrate the return of Lord Rama, Goddess Sita, and Lakshmana to their homeland. From then, Hindus across the globe celebrate the return of the trio as Diwali.

Everyone celebrated the defeat of the arrogant demon-king as it restored the belief that goodness will always triumph over evil. This is the festive spirit of Diwali and it is kept alive even today.

The Rebirth of Lakshmi

Indra, the king of gods and the God of thunder was a great warrior and defeater of multiple evil demons. He was responsible for the protection of Svarga (heaven) and mankind. He was successful in fulfilling his duties and with Goddess Lakshmi's blessings, prosperity and happiness spread to every corner of the world.

Once, Indra disrespected the great sage Durvasa by throwing his offerings to the floor. The disrespect made Goddess Lakshmi very upset and she decided to leave heaven and enter the Milky Ocean (Kshirasagar).

Without the blessings and protection of Lakshmi, the world became gloomy. Crops did not harvest and all the good fortune was lost. People turned greedy, there was no good, and the demons overpowered gods under King Bali's rule. Indra realized it was his mistake that drove the goddess to the depths of the ocean and consulted Lord Vishnu for a solution.

Lord Vishnu gave a thought and came up with a solution. He said that the gods need to churn the Cosmic Ocean to regain Devi Laksmi. However, the Ocean of Milk was a mighty ocean, and stirring it required a lot of power. So the gods decided to team up with demons.

The gods on one side and demons on the other churned the Ocean together with a great effort. They decided to use a massive serpent as a rope in this divine churning. The serpent was weaved around a huge mountain. To keep the mountain straight and upright, Lord Vishnu took the form of a tortoise. The mountain was placed on his shell. The front side of the serpent was held by the demons while the lower half was held by the gods. The churning happened for a thousand years and finally, the Milky Ocean presented its treasures.

The Ocean was a treasure of all things, good and bad. First came on the surface the 14 gems which were divided equally among the gods and demons. From it came the Goddess of misfortune (Jyestha), beautiful and divine female spirits (Apsaras), the wish-granting cow (Kamadhenu), and the god of medicine (Dhanvantri) with a pot of Amrita in his hand, a special magic drink. Anyone who drank Amrita would live forever. The demons and the gods fought over this divine drink.

The demons shouted, "We have helped you gods and we deserve to have the drink before you." The gods summoned Lord Vishnu for help. Lord Vishnu knew that if demons get the ability to live forever, they will harm other creatures. So, he played a trick on the demons.

Lord Vishnu added water to the pot of the drink. Then he changed into his female form Mohini and convinced the demons that they worked harder and should get to drink Amrita first. The divine drink Amrita settled at the bottom of the pot while the water was floating at the top. The demons drank from the pot first, the gods drank after them. So the demons only got the water while the gods got the dense Amrita present at the bottom of the pot. This made the gods stronger than the demons.

The ocean also produced poison. The poison had to be stored somewhere or it could harm everyone. The gods and demons approached Lord Shiva and he swallowed the poison to protect the three worlds.

Finally, the ocean produced Goddess Lakshmi, in all her beauty, standing on a Lotus flower with a golden aura. Everyone bowed down to the goddess of prosperity, wealth, and fertility. Even the demons sang hymns and songs of her praise and glory. Divine elephants came to shower her with flowers and water. The sky started shining and the crops grew. The world flourished and happiness returned to humans.

With Devi Lakshmi and her powers on their side, the gods defeated the demons and again started ruling the entire universe. Goddess Lakshmi is worshipped every year on Diwali with the belief that she comes down on Earth that day. People light clay lamps (diyas) to guide the goddess and even leave their doors unlocked for her to enter their homes. Along with her, she brings prosperity, purity, happiness, and good fortune.

Lord Krishna's Victory

Narkasura was the mighty son of Lord Varaha and Mother Earth. He was the demon king of a city named Pragjyotisha. He was a great and brave warrior and had won many battles. All the kings accepted defeat and Narkasura ruled the entire world. But he was under the association of an evil demon named Banasura. He used his powers in the wrong way and hurt many people.

Once, after winning the whole world, Narkasura had a wish to defeat the gods. He said, "Now that the world is ours, let us advance to heaven (Swargaloka)."
But his ministers reminded him that he cannot live forever like the gods and the gods have an unfair advantage. He realized that to overpower all the gods, he needed to be eternal.

He then went to the forest and started meditating on Lord Brahma. He worshipped him day and night for many years until one day Lord Brahma appeared before him. Narkasura was busy in his prayers when he heard a soft but powerful voice.

"I am very happy with your worship, my child," Lord Brahma said.

Narkasura looked up and then bowed down to pay respects to the god.

"Stand up, child. Ask for one boon and I shall grant it," offered Lord Brahma.

Narkasura said, "My dear Lord, please make me immortal. Give me a blessing that I will live forever."

Such a blessing cannot be given and Brahma had to turn Narkasura down. He instead asked him to wish for something else.

"Lord, give me the boon that only my mother can defeat me," finally he answered.

Brahma granted him this boon
and disappeared.

With the blessing that only his mother can overpower him, Narkasura started marching toward heaven (Swargaloka) with his army. They reached the palace of the mighty God of Thunder and the king of gods, Indra. Indra fought against him but he soon understood that he cannot beat Narkasura. He rushed to the savior, Lord Vishnu for help. Vishnu knew the matter and advised Indra to talk to Lord Krishna. Krishna was a human incarnation (avatar) of Lord Vishnu. Without a delay, he landed on Earth.

Meanwhile, Narkasura captured all the people of Indra's palace and trapped all women in his palace. In Krishna's palace, Indra begged Lord Krishna to do something about Narakasura. When he heard about trapped people from upset Indra, Lord Krishna's wife Devi Satyabhama exclaimed, "My Lord, this cannot wait. We have to stop the demon from hurting more people!"

Krishna said, "Yes, my queen. I will prepare the chariot and go to fight the demon right this moment!"

Satyabhama insisted on coming with him. She was a warrior herself and wanted to ride the chariot for Krishna. So, Lord Krishna and Satyabhama flew to Indra's palace.

On seeing the couple approach him, Narkasura laughed.

"You have brought a woman to a battlefield, O Krishna? You underestimate me so much!" exclaimed Narkasura.

On hearing these words, Satyabhama got furious and asked Krishna to enter the battlefield. A fierce fight took place between the two warriors. Divine weapons were used and Narkasura's army was getting smaller and smaller. Even though he fought bravely, Lord Krishna got hurt. He fell to the ground and passed out.

Satyabhama looked at Narkasura with great fury and roared, "How dare you hurt my husband this way?"

Saying this, she used Lord Krishna's divine weapon and defeated Narkasura. Narkasura got hurt and fell to the ground. At that same time, Lord Krishna rose from the ground and bowed to Devi Satyabhama. In that final moment, Narkasura realized that Satyabhama was an avatar of his mother, Bhudevi, Mother Earth.

He joined both his hands and asked for forgiveness. Then Lord Krishna and Satyabhama rescued all the people that Narkasura had kidnapped.

This day is celebrated as the Narak Chaturdashi, one day before Diwali and it signifies the victory of good over evil, however strong the evil is. Every year on this day, we seek blessings from God for the strength to fight against all the evil around us.

Kali Destroys Demons

The world was flourishing and the gods were at peace. Nature blossomed and birds sang songs of joy. But one day the demons wanted to fight and destroy the peace and gods.

Shumbh and Nishumbh were evil demons and wanted to rule over the gods. Indra was the king of gods and ruled heaven. Evil demons entered Indra's palace and started fighting the gods. Due to a blessing, the gods could not defeat the brothers, and Shumbh and Nishumbh became stronger.

All the gods fled the palace and took shelter in Mount Kailash, the heavenly place of Lord Shiva and Goddess Parvati. Goddess Parvati asked them:

"What is the matter? Why are all of you here?"
"O Goddess, please save us! Shumbh and Nishumbh are harming all the gods of Indraloka and now, they're chasing us!"

Goddess Parvati said, "Do not fear, O mighty gods! Let the demons come here and I will handle them."

When the demons reached Mount Kailash, Goddess Parvati stepped forward and demanded, "Go back and stop harming others!"

The brothers laughed and yelled, "A woman! Fighting us! Try to defeat us lady and you will fail miserably."

With that, the brothers attacked the goddess. She shielded herself and fought them bravely. In the process, Mother Parvati took her warrior form, Goddess Durga. Durga was more fierce and defeated the demons easily.

Word got out and the other demon named Raktabeej was enraged. He hurried to Mount Kailash and saw all the gods with Goddess Durga. He howled an evil roar and challenged, "You foolish gods! How dare you hurt my brother demons? Now you have to fight me!"

Raktabeej was a great devotee of Lord Brahma. Once he prayed to Brahma for many years and Lord Brahma asked him to wish for something. Raktabeej wished for a unique blessing. Whenever he is hurt on a battlefield, new versions of Raktabeej will be created.

Goddess Durga was unaware of this blessing and attacked the demon. She was successful in wounding the demon but many more demons appeared. This angered Goddess Durga. Raktabeej laughed and attacked all the gods and Durga.

Goddess Durga had to stop the demon from hurting more people and attacked him again. But with every blow, the number of Raktabeej kept on multiplying. A whole army full of Raktabeej was created and all of them started harming other gods. Durga became so angry that she howled a frightening scream.

The earth trembled from her scream and her body turned black. Her eyes turned red and she looked at the demon with anger. This form of Goddess Parvati is known as Goddess Kali. Kali is the most powerful feminine form, filled with anger and might. She is known to maintain the balance of nature. In Sanskrit, Kali means time, and her form represents the beginning and end of time.

The demons around her disappeared with the anger of the goddess. Some fled away. She chased the army of demons and defeated them, one by one. With every victory, her anger grew. When she defeated the last Raktabeej, her rage became uncontrollable. She started overpowering and destroying everything that came in her way. The sky turned black and the clouds thundered.

This scared the gods and they rushed to Lord Shiva, pleading for help. Lord Shiva was also scared to stop his wife in this state of anger. He sighed and ran in the direction of Goddess Kali. On seeing her so angry, he silently lay down on the ground and held his breath.

In anger, Goddess Kali stepped on him but suddenly realized what she had done. Lord Shiva absorbed and neutralized all the anger that was within Goddess Kali and she returned to her original form.

This day is celebrated one day before Diwali as 'Kali Chaudas'. It shows us the power a mother takes when her children are in danger. On this day, people seek Mother Kali's blessings to destroy the evil around them and always protect them the way she protected the gods from the evil demons.

The Legend of King Bali

The great demon king Bali was the grandson of king Prahlada. Despite being a demon he was a good king. His kingdom flourished under his rule and the people were happy. He was kind, generous, and thoughtful. Stories of his bravery, justice, and devotion spread to all corners of the world. He was a great devotee of Lord Vishnu and had his blessings.

But the other demons were not like him. They constantly attacked heaven and hurt the gods. After many such incidents, the gods decided that they will wage a war against the demons. But fighting the demons meant fighting against Bali. They knew Bali couldn't be defeated without Lord Vishnu's assistance. They ran to Lord Vishnu's palace and asked his assistance against King Bali and the demons.

Lord Vishnu finally said, "I understand your situation but Bali is a righteous king and my devotee. I will not fight against him unless he does something wrong."

Indra, the king of gods, pleaded, "But Lord, we are being attacked by the demons again and again. Please show us another way to put a stop to this."

Vishnu had declined to fight against King Bali in battle but there was a way to end this story non-violently. He said, "Okay Indra. Leave it to me to defeat Bali."

King Bali was very generous and he was preparing for a ritual offering (Yajna). The offering was done to show gratitude. He had declared that he will donate anything a person asks for after the sacred offering. The sacrifice was successful and King Bali was giving charity generously.

A dwarf entered the sacred area with a small umbrella and smiled at the king.

The dwarf exclaimed, "Hail, O king of the three worlds!" He was Lord Vishnu in the form of a dwarf named Vamana. King Bali welcomed him.

"Demand anything you want, boy! Cows, food, villages, wealth. Anything you demand will be yours," announced the king.

"O king, I am a simple man. What will I do of these things?" asked Vamana in return.

"But now that you have entered the sacred ground, you have to ask for something," explained Bali.

King Bali's guru Shukracharya called him to a side.

"O king, do not give this boy anything! He is not who he seems," said Shukracharya. "I know, Gurudev. How can I not recognize the Almighty? And who am I to turn him down? I will give all I have to him happily," the great devotee Bali replied.

He went straight to Vamana and asked him again.
Vamana finally demanded, "I do not want more than I need, great king. All I ask is the property right over the land that my 3 steps can cover." King Bali smiled and readily said yes to him.

The dwarf Vamana grew to enormous size and covered the entire placed his foot on Earth. For the second step, Vamana chose Heaven. While he was thinking of land for his third step, King Bali rushed and offered himself to the Lord.

"Oh Lord Vishnu, I know it is you. Bless me by allowing me to serve you for the rest of my life."

Vamana smiled and placed his feet on Bali. As a result, Bali was pushed down into the underworld (Paatal Lok). Lord Vishnu also gave him the boon to come to Earth once every year. He became the king of Paatal Lok and ruled there with the same bravery he ruled on Earth. The gods lived happily while King Bali was safe in the underworld, so gods can defeat evil demons. Everyone was happy.

People believe that King Bali visits Earth every year on the day after Diwali and it is celebrated as 'Bali Pratipada'. People in the Southern part of India worship Bali every Diwali and celebrate his homecoming. People even make clay idols of the king to commemorate his bravery, devotion, and generosity.

Pandavas & Their Evil Brothers (Mahabharata)

Once upon a time, there was an ancient city of Hastinapura that had a history of the greatest kings. Two princes were growing up under the guidance of their grandfather Bhishma. The elder brother was Dhritrashtra and the younger one was Pandu. Dhritrashtra can't see by birth. Since he was blind, when the time came, Pandu was made the king.

Both the brothers got married to beautiful princesses and started living happily. Pandu had five sons, Yudhishthira, Bheema, Arjuna, Nakula, and Sahadeva. The five brothers were called 'Pandavas'. Dhritrashtra bore 100 sons and a daughter. He named his eldest son Duryodhana and his second eldest son Dushasana. The 101 children of Dhritrashtra were called 'Kauravas'.

The princes grew up in the palace and gained knowledge from the royal Guru Drona and their grandfather Bhishma. Due to some reasons and poor health, King Pandu couldn't rule Hastinapura for long and Dhritrashtra became the new king of Hastinapura.

Even though Dhritrashtra was the king, Yudhishthira, Pandu's eldest son, was more capable of the throne and everyone else thought so too. So, they all came up with the decision that Yudhisthira should be made a crown prince. But Duryodhana, the eldest Kaurava was jealous and enraged. He did not accept Yudhisthira as the king.

He demanded to his father, "His father Pandu was your younger brother and he was still made the king, just because you can't see! That was an injustice. As your elder son, I should be the king. I will not give that thrown up just because my father is blind!"

33

Duryodhana's anger grew every minute and he demanded to have half of the city of Hastinapura. Yudhisthira accepted this suggestion and Hastinapura was divided into two parts.

But after some time, Duryodhana was jealous of Pandava's prosperity. He asked his uncle Shakuni to plan something to get the other half too. This uncle was a cheater and a master gambler. He suggested inviting the Pandavas to a game of gambling. The Pandavas agreed to it, thinking it was an effort of Kauravas to strengthen their bond.

In the game, the Pandavas lost everything. They lost their empire, their wealth, and their weapons. They even lost themselves and wife Draupadi*. They sat with their heads hanging in shame.

Duryodhan laughed, "This is exactly how you should always be! Ashamed and penniless!"

He insulted them and then started to insult Draupadi. He ordered his brother Dushasana to drag Draupadi to the court. She was insulted and no one but the wicked Kauravas enjoyed her disrespect.

---

* The Pandavas married Draupadi together because their mother accidentally ordered the brothers to divide amongst themselves whatever they received (Draupadi). Also, Draupadi had asked for a boon to have a husband who is the best king, mightiest, best archer, most handsome, and most patient. These qualities were not humanly possible to be possessed by one man and so, due to the boon, Draupadi had to marry the Pandavas.

An angry Draupadi asked for justice and king Dhritrashtra ordered Duryodhana to give whatever he got in the unfair game. Duryodhana refused right that moment. His uncle Shakuni came up with a solution. He said, "O king, Duryodhana isn't wrong. Why will anyone want to give back what they've won? But something can be done. The Pandavas will have to go into exile for 13 years and lead a normal life. After that, they shall spend one year in disguise. If we recognize even one of them, they will have to repeat their exile and disguise exile."

The Pandavas accepted this suggestion. They spent 13 years in the forest, working hard. Meanwhile, Duryodhana misused his power and hurt the people of Hastinapura. For the last year, the Pandavas took shelter in King Virata's kingdom. They all worked as servants in the king's palace and were successful in hiding their identities for one entire year.

Since the Kauravas were unsuccessful in finding them in the last year of their exile, The Pandavas returned to Hastinapura to demand their kingdom. Duryodhana was not satisfied and refused to give any land to the brothers. Lord Krishna also requested Duryodhana to give the Pandavas five villages. Lord Krishna requested, "Give them five villages, only five villages, O brother and the Pandavas will not complain."

But arrogant Duryodhana declined. Wife Draupadi was enraged and wanted revenge. After a lot of requests, when the Kauravas denied peace, Lord Krishna suggested that war was the only option. Lord Krishna promised that he will not fight, will not touch any weapon but will ride the chariot for his friend and the third Pandava, Arjuna.

The great war between brothers began. On the first day of the war, all the warriors stood on the battlefield with weapons in their hands. The war was fought between the sons of two loving brothers and their relatives. Arjuna saw his grandfather and Guru Drona against him and he dropped his weapons.

Arjuna said, "O Krishna, I see my family members on the other side. I know brother Duryodhana has done wrong but I cannot fight him, or grandfather Bhishma, or Gurudev (Guru Drona) for a piece of land! What will I do of the kingdom, Krishna, when I will not have my kin and loved ones to celebrate the victory with?"

Then Lord Krishna narrated Bhagavad Geeta (the song of God) to him. He explained to him his duty as a husband, as a warrior. He said to Arjuna that despite his bonds with anyone, it is his duty to fight for justice and goodness. Arjuna understood his life's meaning and duty and was prepared to fight the evil side.

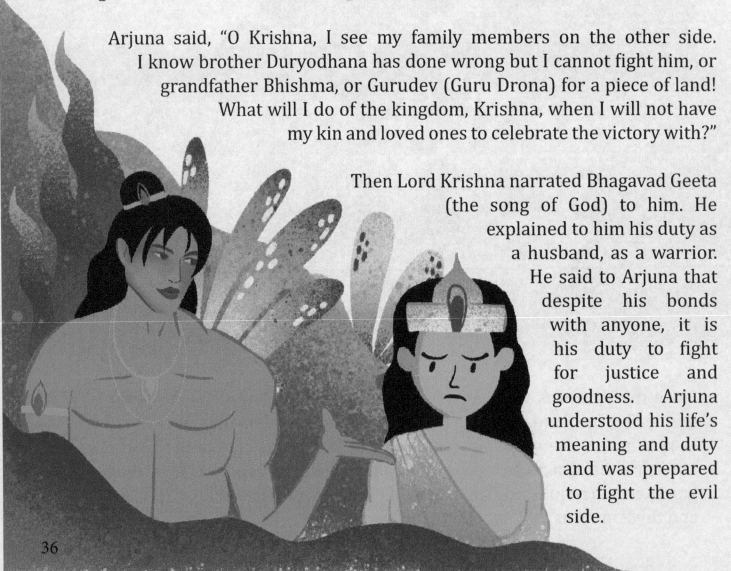

The great war took place for 18 days and in the end, the Pandavas won.
All the 100 Kaurava brothers were defeated.

When Pandavas returned to their homeland, victorious and satisfied, the people of Hastinapura were overjoyed. They lit every part of Hastinapura with clay lamps (diyas) and shared sweets. Dharma (righteousness, justice, and goodness) returned to Hastinapura. With this tale, Lord Krishna explained that nothing is more important than duty, and that good will always triumph over evil.

Diwali is not just about lighting diyas and making sweets, it brings joy in a lot more ways. This part of the book contains 6 stories and all six tales will boost the spirit of the festival in your children. Diwali is a vast festival, the rituals and traditions may differ but do not let differences affect its beauty and spirit.

Diwali is a festival of 5 days and all days have different meanings. The first five tales will show the celebration of each day and the last one is a happy tale of love and unity. We hope your children rejoice in the warm light and sweet treats Diwali brings!

Diwali
Celebrations

Ahana Celebrates Dhanteras

Ahana woke up to the sound of melodious hymns and the sound of dangling bells. It was Dhanteras, the first day of Diwali and she was very excited about the festival. Every year on Diwali, Ahana and her parents spent a lot of quality time together and enjoyed all the rituals with close family friends.

"Wake up, my dear. Diwali begins today and you know that we always wake early on festivals, don't we?" said her dad. Ahana smiled. She gave a warm hug to her dad and wished him, "Happy Dhanteras, dad!"

"Where's mom?" Ahana asked.

"She is cleaning the altar, dear. And after that, she will go to the temple. Will you go with her?" Ahana's father asked her.

"Yes, dad. I will bathe quickly and be ready in 10 minutes."

She chose her traditional clothes and her favorite slippers. When her mother saw Ahana, she said, "Oh my dear, you look beautiful! Happy Dhanteras!" Ahana wished her back and started collecting the things she wants to take to the temple. In a small orange basket, she put a copper pot with some milk, some oil, one diya, incense sticks, and sandalwood.

"Thank you for helping me out dear but we need to make some rangoli before we leave for the temple," Ahana's mother said.
"No problem, mom. Let's make the rangoli together."

They ground some soaked rice and made a white paste. This white paste was used to make beautiful and symmetric geometrical patterns in front of the house. While making the patterns on the floor, Ahana asked her mother,
"But mom, why do we use rice flour?"
"My dear, it is an age-old practice to feed the ants, birds, and other small creatures. It also denotes purity and wellness."

After putting the rangoli, they both walk to the temple holding each other's hands.

Ahana always liked spending time in the temple. It had a cold marble floor and a beautiful dome. Whenever they came to the temple, Ahana's mom always picked her up to ring the bell on the top. She felt calm and peaceful in the temple every day but it looked even better during festivals. At festivals, people came to decorate the temple in beautiful colors. She met a lot of people who had lit many diyas in the temple. Even in broad daylight, the temple looked brighter than it always did.

After they visited the temple, Ahana and her mother visited the market for some festive shopping. They paid a visit to the goldsmith and bought a small gold coin. "Why do we buy this on Dhanteras?" curious little Ahana asked.

The goldsmith explained, "Buying a new metal on Dhanteras, especially gold, increases the positivity and prosperity the festival brings."

Ahana smiled at the kind goldsmith and thanked him for explaining. Her mother then took her to a small idol shop. There, Ahana was surprised to see so many delicate but beautiful and colorful idols. There were idols of Goddess Lakshmi, Lord Ganesha, Goddess Saraswati, Lord Vishnu, Lord Durga, and many more deities. Ahana couldn't decide which one was the best because every idol was better than the last.

"Namaste, we need clay idols of Mother Lakshmi and Lord Ganesha," Ahana's mother said to the vendor.

Ahana knew this ritual and was always very fond of it. Every year, the family welcomed new idols of Lord Ganesha and Goddess Lakshmi and dipped the old idols in water. Her mother said this represents the cycle of life. After dissolving, she poured the muddy water into the plants. This gives them more nourishing soil.

"Brother, are these idols made of real mud and clay? Will they dissolve in water?" asked her mother.
"Yes, sister. They all are soluble in water. Also, they have a seed in them so that when you dissolve the idols and water your plants with them, a new life grows," the vendor replied.
"That's wonderful! Please pack one of each for us," her mother said.

After reaching, the whole family cleaned their home. The windows were wiped and cupboards were dusted.

After a full day of cleaning and shopping, in the evening, sweet melodious hymns were played. Family switched on the lanterns that were hung outside their windows and balconies and enjoy a tasty and healthy dinner.

Dhanteras is celebrated to worship Dhanvantri, god of medicine and health, and Kubera, god of wealth to explain that health, safety, and love are the real wealth.

A Day Full of Diwali Preparations

Ryan was a sweet and creative boy. He enjoyed his art class the most and playing with colors was his favorite hobby. One day he came home from school and his mother called, "Welcome back, dear. Look what I have brought for you!"

Ryan followed his mother and saw a big basket of flowers, mango leaves, and pom-poms. He knew what this meant. Diwali was close and they will make a lot of home decorations together.

"Wow, I was missing this mom! Let's make the Torana," an excited Ryan exclaimed.

Together, they sewed flowers and mango leaves in a big garland called Torana. During this time, they both talked and shared many stories.

"Good job, Ryan. We will hang this on the front door so that we welcome people into our home with happy fragrance."

Ryan was overjoyed with his work. His mother said, "There are more fun things for today, son."

"Wow, what are they, mom?" His mother brought a container of clay lamps (diyas) and pots. All of them were wet like they've been washed a few minutes ago.

"I soaked them in water because otherwise they absorb oil and paint a lot. We can keep them in sunlight, and when they're dry, we can color them!" exclaimed his mother.

Ryan was very happy. Painting diyas and pots are his favorite activities. Every Diwali he painted many diyas. He always looked forward to this part of Diwali- painting and decorating diya as he wants. Together, they spread the diyas in the sun and then had lunch together.

When they were dry, Ryan and his mother picked them up carefully and started painting them. Along with colors, they also decorated diyas with beads, sea shells, mirror pieces, and glitter. While decorating diyas, Ryan's mother told him the story of Diwali and how Mother Lakshmi follows all the colorful and bright diyas on Diwali.

All the diyas looked lovely and at last Ryan painted the big pots alone. There were two beautiful pots. He drew a peacock on one pot with chalk, painted it, and decorated it very gracefully. For the second one, he painted small detailed patterns on the pot and made it very colorful.

After the decoration, Ryan volunteered to help his mother in making Diwali delicacies. He enjoyed the process of making sweets and spending quality time with his mother.

They first made balls for gulab jamun. Then his mother friend it and they put the balls in the rose-flavored sugar syrup they had prepared. Then they prepared Karanji, small puffs filled with dry coconut, dry fruits, nuts, and sugar. His mother then fried the puffs and they stored all the tasty Diwali treats in boxes

In the evening, Ryan's father came home. He bought a big box with him. Ryan asked his parents if he could open the box and they said yes. In the box was a beautiful orange lantern. It was a DIY set and Ryan begged to make the lantern immediately.

They constructed together a lovely lantern which they hung in their living room window. His father had also brought three strings of bright fairy lights for other windows. The fairy lights were used to decorate the room windows and the kitchen window.

Then they had a tasty dinner. After the dinner, Ryan proudly showed his father all the diyas and pots he had decorated. He also showed the Torana which he had carefully placed on the center table. His dad was very impressed and kissed him. After that, they enjoyed some Diwali treats that Ryan and his mother had prepared.

Every year, Ryan's father applied henna to his mother's palms. Following the ritual, before going to bed, the three of them talked about their busy and good day while Ryan's father applied henna onto Ryan's mother's hands. Ryan insisted on joining his father since he loved drawing and painting. Ryan drew on his mother's left hand while his father drew on her right.

The family kissed each other good night and went to bed excited for the grand festival of Diwali. Ryan always cherishes the five days of Diwali because of all the fun, art, and love the festival brings.

Shalvi Celebrates Lakshmi Pooja

"Wake up dear, it's time to have a bath," Shalvi's mom screamed.
"But mom it's just 8 a.m.!" complained Shalvi.
"My dear, it's Diwali. You always wake up early at festivals and help mama, don't you? Come on, we'll have treats after the work is finished."

That woke Shalvi up. She got ready in just a few minutes and went into the living room.

"Good morning, princess," her grandfather greeted her as soon as she stepped out of her bedroom.
"Good morning, pa!" She ran and gave her grandpa a hug.
"I see my little princess is ready so early today. Happy Diwali!"
"Happy Diwali!" By now, Shalvi was in a good mood. She asked her mother for breakfast but her grandpa stopped her. He ordered her to touch her mother's feet.
"But why pa?"
"Shalvi dear, your mama always feeds us, helps you study, keeps us happy, and brings joy to the entire house. She is the Lakshmi of our house. Today, we worship Goddess Lakshmi as the goddess and source of wealth, health, knowledge, and prosperity. And what better way to start your day than to seek the blessings of our Lakshmi, eh?"

Shalvi nodded her head and went to touch her mother's feet. "Thank you for everything you do, mama."

Then Shalvi insisted on hanging the Torana on the front door herself. She called her father and said, "Dada, can you please help me hang it up there?"

Her father picked Shalvi up and they hung the Torana together. A Torana is a garland of fresh marigold flowers and mango leaves that makes the front door very welcoming. They then washed the nameplate and hung them back too.

It was a family ritual for everyone to cook together. Shalvi's grandpa kneaded the dough for puris, her mother cut vegetables, and Shalvi was wiping the wet dishes while her father was near the stove, making the curry. The house was filled with a rich aroma of Indian food as they all prepared dishes filled with healthy and tasty spices.

After they prepared the lunch, a small portion of every dish was put in a dish. The dish was filled with puris, kachoris, Indian curries, dal, rice, pickle, salad, and kheer. This lunch plate was offered to the gods. After they made the offering, they had lunch. Festive Indian meals are just delightful.

In the afternoon, Shalvi decorated the plate for pooja with flower petals and red tilak, and turmeric. She then made a beautiful rangoli in front of the main door with the colored powder grandpa had brought for her. She made many flowers, diyas, and a lantern in the rangoli. Then she and her grandpa made cotton wicks to light diyas in the evening.

She helped her mother make holy offerings or prasadam. Prasadam is a substance that we believe has been eaten by God and is thus blessed. By eating a small portion of prasadam, people believe that they become blessed and immune to problems. Shalvi's mother mixed some milk with cashews, raisins, almonds, sugar, and ghee to make a thick liquid. This liquid called Panchamrita is the main prasadam and the gods love this sweet and healthy drink.

Time went by fast and it was already evening. Shalvi, like always, switched on the lights of all the lanterns and lights that decorated their windows. When she looked out of her window, she could see many other windows decorated with lights and lanterns and this made her very happy. Then, Shalvi and other family members changed into the new Diwali clothes.

It was time to do the pooja. They all cleaned the part of the living room near the home altar again. Incense sticks were burnt to fill the altar with fragrance. Then mother filled oil in all the diyas and her father told her to bring all her books. He placed the books near a photo of Goddess Lakshmi and Lord Ganesha. It was a beautiful picture where Goddess Lakshmi was sitting on a lotus with elephants on both her sides and Lord Ganesha was sitting on a throne with a book and a laddoo. Everyone sat down near the photo of the gods and chanted holy mantras. They sang songs of the glory of Mother Lakshmi and Lord Ganesha.

They worshipped all the books. When she asked why, grandpa said, "Dear, books give us knowledge and wisdom. So, worshipping our books is important."

Shalvi's father tied a sacred red thread around his wrist to protect himself from evil spirits. Her mother told her to pray for anything she wants to the goddess of prosperity, wealth, and purity, Mother Lakshmi. "Pray with true faith and Mother Lakshmi will listen to you, dear," she said.

Then all the diyas were lit and placed on a plate. Then they all placed a diya in their rooms and kitchen and near the windows. Shalvi took four diyas and placed them on the corners of her rangoli. After that, they decorated the front of the door with more diyas. They were all colorful and lit every part of their home.

Then the family went outdoors to burst some crackers. Every Diwali night, the family walked to see lanterns decorating the neighborhood. Even though the moon wasn't there, the sky was lit with sparkling fireworks. They all went to the terrace of their house and watched fireworks from there. Shalvi was surprised but pleased to see all the glittering light in the sky.

When Shalvi was sitting in her grandpa's lap and watching the fireworks, her father brought another lantern for her. She was a bit confused but her father guided her through it. It was a cloth lantern that fled in the sky. They lit the cloth lantern and set it free in the sky. The balloon lantern floated up and up in the sky.

"Think Shalvi, how many people will look for the moon and will see this one small lantern. They will be so happy! When I was little, I used to set diyas in the river with many other people," said Shalvi's mother.
"But mom, why do we do all this?" curious Shalvi asked.
"To light every part of the world we can, honey. Diwali is all about spreading light wherever darkness exists, isn't it?"

Shalvi nodded. She had celebrated a day full of lights and color, filled with sweetness and joy. She thanked and prayed to Goddess Lakshmi to keep everyone happy and healthy forever.

Roofie & Jay

Jay loved animals and birds. He was very fond of his little pet puppy, Roofie. Every morning Jay and Roofie would go out for a walk in the park. The park was far from their home but Roofie gave him good company which made the walk fun. Roofie was very friendly and in the park, a lot of children played with him. They threw a big stick to the other side of the park and Roofie always chased to catch the stick.

It was a bright sunny day and Jay had celebrated Diwali just a day ago. To celebrate the importance of Roofie as a family member, Jay's parents had put a red Tilak on his forehead, just like they put on Jay's forehead. Jay was very happy and exclaimed, "That makes us siblings!"

After the walk at the park, Jay went to school. The school was fun and he even got an A on his test. He was excited to tell this news to his parents. He held the test paper in his fist and ran back home excitedly.

Every day whenever Jay came close to his house, Roofie would start barking with thrill. But this time Jay could hear no barking. He came closer to his house and even called out for Roofie.

"Roofie, I'm home!" he yelled but there was no response. Jay got scared.

He ran to his mother and asked, "Mama, where is Roofie? Is he sleeping?" His mother was confused. She said she didn't know and yelled for the little puppy but she didn't get any response. Jay searched every corner of the house but he couldn't find him. He started crying.

"Mama, we need to go find him. He might be in trouble."
"Don't make haste, dear. Let papa come and we will go find him, okay? Freshen up."

An upset Jay changed into a fresh set of clothes and sat on his bed. He didn't even want to show his mother the test paper on which he got an A. Then the doorbell rang and he ran, hoping that it will be someone with Roofie. He opened the door and his father was standing in the front. He saw how sad Jay was and he asked him about the matter. Jay said everything to him and he said, "Let us go and ask the neighbors, son. They might have seen our Roofie."

Jay's father set out to ask everyone around the block. He asked all the neighbors but no one knew where the little puppy was. By this time, it had started to rain now.

In the end, he said, "Dear son, that was the last house in the neighborhood and no one knows where Roofie is. Let's file a complaint with the police and go back home."

They filed a missing complaint and go back home.

There, his mother had prepared a very delicious dinner for Jay but he was very sad.

"We couldn't find Roofie, mama. No one has seen him today."

Seeing her son upset, Jay's mother decided to tell him a story. "Come here, son. Let's hear a story."

A sad Jay walked up to her and his mother wrapped her arms around him. His father also sat next to them.

"Do you know why I have prepared so many dishes today?

Jay shook his head to say no. He looked over to the dining table and sure enough, he saw a lot of dishes.

"Today is Govardhan Pooja. Just like today, many years ago, it was raining heavily in Gokul. Lord Indra, the god of rain and thunder was unhappy with the people of Gokul and he flooded the city. All houses were ruined, and people couldn't find shelter. They all cried and begged for mercy but angry Indra didn't stop. It kept raining.

At that time, Lord Krishna was a kid, almost of your age. He was growing up with his brother in Gokul. Being the Almighty, he knew everything. He told his mama and papa to take everyone to Mount Govardhan, the largest mountain in the village. Everyone was surprised but they followed little Krishna's advice. All the villagers started walking up to the mountain.

There, on reaching, Lord Krishna lifted the entire mountain on his palm. Everyone was surprised. Then little Krishna declared, "O villagers, please get under the mountain to save yourselves from the thunder and rain."

Everyone took shelter under the mountain. Krishna was still a child then and wasn't very tall. To give more height, Krishna carried the entire mountain on his little finger. To help him, other villagers brought sticks and supported the mountain base on them. That night, food was cooked under Mount Govardhan, and to mark this important day, every year, one day after Diwali, we make a lot of dishes to thank God for everything we have, in health and safety."

"Oh, Lord Krishna saved all the people," cried Jay.

"Yes, and he will save Roofie too."

"No mama, we can't be sure that he is safe," Jay protested.

"Yes honey, but we have to pray that he is. Remember, Lord Krishna always protects his beloved devotees and listens to their prayers. In his own ways, he makes sure everything and everyone is alright, dear," his mother explains.

Jay was sad but he went to bed sobbing and praying to Lord Krishna. It was raining heavily and he was scared for his little puppy. "Please keep him safe, Krishna," he kept repeating. In a few minutes, he fell asleep.

The next morning, he woke up when his mother called him. "Jay, look who is here," she screamed.

Rubbing his eyes, he went into the living room when he was attacked by Roofie with kisses. He was so happy, he started crying. He looked up to see a friend from the park, Ron.

Ron said, "I saw the little pup near my house and started playing with him. But then it started raining. I realized you weren't there, mate and that the pup was alone. Then I took him to my house. He was missing you but I couldn't bring him last night due to the rain. I'm sorry, " Ron said.

"Oh no, Ron. You have been of great help. Thanks for keeping my Roofie safe in the rain. He is so small, I got scared for him," a relieved Jay said.

Jay's mother asked, "Boys, would you like some Diwali sweets now that everyone is safe and happy?"

They all enjoyed sweets and Ron carried some for his little sister too. Jay understood the real meaning of faith and thanked Lord Krishna for always looking over his devotees.

Brother and Sister Reunite on Bhaidooj

Just a day after Diwali, Sasha, and her family packed their bags to visit her aunt and uncle. Sasha loved the Diwali holidays as all her relatives brought her gifts and sweets. But this Diwali was different. They were going to visit her aunt whom she had never met before.

On the way, Sasha asked, "Dadda, who is this new aunt?"

Her father patted her lovingly and said, "Little one, we are visiting my sister first time after your birth. She hasn't seen you in person but she loves you dearly."

Sasha was excited to meet her aunt. The next morning, they left home early. After a long and tiring journey, they reached her aunt's home at 11 a.m.

Sasha had never seen her dad so excited. He was smiling to himself. They reached an apartment and rang the doorbell. A beautiful woman opened the door. She was in utter shock when she saw Sasha and her parents. The woman started crying and surprisingly, Sasha's father started crying too.

Sasha was very confused. She wanted to go ask what was wrong but then she saw her mother. Her mother was beaming with a smile and tears in her eyes. Sasha's uncle welcomed everyone inside the house.

"Brother, it has been 8 years since we last met," the woman finally said in a happy voice. She knew this was her aunt because she looked a lot like her father.

"Yes sister, I wanted to come so much but couldn't. Forgive me," cried her father.

"It's of no matter, brother. You are here, on Bhaidooj, and it is all that matters!" exclaimed the lady. Then she hugged Sasha's mother and Sasha. She offered the family some sweets and water. They all talked for a few minutes when Sasha's aunt said, "Brother, Sister, freshen up. Let me celebrate Bhaidooj properly this time!"

Sasha was very confused. She didn't know what Bhaidooj meant but following her aunt's orders, she took a quick shower and got dressed in a beautiful lehenga. Then her aunt asked for Sasha's help in decorating the Prayer plate. With petals of various flowers, turmeric powder, and sandal powder, she made the entire plate colorful. Then her aunt placed four pieces of sweet, a small bowl of curd, some grains of rice, and some more sandalwood powder on the plate. They both then went into the living room where Sasha's mother and father were already waiting.

"Aunt, what is Bhaidooj?" Sasha asked her aunt.
"Dear, we celebrate Bhaidooj, or the beautiful bond of a brother and sister a day after Diwali. On this day, sisters apply tilak on their brother's foreheads, giving them their blessings of safety and prosperity. In return, brothers give their sisters a present," her aunt explained.

Sasha's aunt then called her father to sit on a chair. She lit up a beautiful diya and placed it on the plate too. Then Sasha's aunt moved the prayer plate in circular directions in front of her father's face a few times. After doing that, she kept the plate on the table nearby and put a red sandalwood powder Tilak on his forehead. She fed a sweet to him and in return, Sasha's father gave her aunt a present. Her aunt was very excited and she opened the package carefully. In the box were 8 different pouches. On every pouch, her father had written a year.

Sasha's aunt was confused but open the oldest one. It was a beaded bracelet. In the second pouch, she found a small locket with a beautiful pink crystal-studded in it. Then she opened the third pouch and in it were 4 bangles. In the next five pouches were a beaded necklace, a bracelet with coral shells, a pair of paper earrings, and a gold and silver necklace. To Sasha, these looked like some cheap jewelry but her aunt's eyes lit up when she saw all of them. She almost cried and kept saying, "You remembered!"

"Of course, I remembered, sister. Just like you remembered to cook all my favorite dishes although you didn't know I was visiting," her father replied.

Sasha was confused and asked, "What are you talking about, dad and aunt?"

Her aunt smiled. "Honey, as kids we didn't have enough money. We tried to save some but I saw that your father tried his best. I loved jewelry from my childhood and I once demanded your father to only give me jewelry that he makes with his hands.

"He used to pick every crystal or beautiful stone or sea shell to make something different every year. If he couldn't find anything different, he'd make me a piece of beaded jewelry. For all the years that we couldn't celebrate Bhaidooj together, my brother always remembered to make my jewelry. He didn't even miss a year!" she cried.

Sasha was so proud of all the jewelry her father had made for his sister. They enjoyed some more Diwali snacks and talked for hours about their lives. Sasha saw a deep bond between her aunt and her father and wished to have a brother to share such a beautiful bond.

Sasha's mother always said that Diwali celebrates every bond, every person and now she can truly see it.

Tanya and Rita Celebrate Together

Tanya studied in first grade. She was very sweet and obedient. Her parents were very happy with their daughter. The family always dined together and talked about their day.

One day when they were having dinner together, Tanya's father said, "Tanya, your mama said you helped her with the Diwali cleaning. You also helped your mama make Diwali sweets. That is very good, my child. So, as a reward, you can ask for anything you want."

Tanya was overjoyed. She said, "Mom, Dad, I always wanted that fancy bicycle that Maria rides. The one with glitter paint! And I want a new Aladdin bag and a magic pen. The ink just vanishes and my friends use it to trick each other!"
"Very well, my dear. You will get all this. We will go this Sunday," her mom said.
"Why Sunday? We can go shopping today!"
"Yes, dear but Diwali starts on Sunday. And do you know what the first day of Diwali is?"
Tanya shook her head.
"Tanya, the first day of Diwali is celebrated as Dhanteras. It is when you buy new things that make you happy or wealthy."
"This is such a fun festival!"
"Yes, it is good but it is not just about shopping. The celebration is for 5 days and the first one is to buy things that make you happy!"

68

Tanya eagerly waited for Dhanteras. One day, her best friend Maria did not come to school. Tanya was sitting alone when she saw that another girl was sitting alone, too. She asked her if she could join her and the girl said yes. Tanya knew this girl. Her name was Rita and she lived a block away from Tanya's house. She was a shy kid and nobody talked to her. But when she talked to her, they became friends instantly. They talked a lot during lunch break and Tanya was so excited that she told Rita about the things she will get on Dhanteras.

Rita was very happy. She said, "That's amazing Tanya! Your choice is so good!"

Then Tanya asked Rita, "So what are you asking for Dhanteras?"
Rita fell silent. She looked at the floor. Tanya thought she had said something very wrong.
"I'm sorry to upset you, Rita," Tanya apologized.
"Oh no, you didn't upset me. I wanted a Barbie bag this year as my old one has worn out."

Indeed, Rita's bag looked very old and ragged. Rita continued, "But I don't ask my mother for anything. She works really hard to give me everything she can. I don't want to upset her by asking more."
Tanya fell silent.
"Once I ask her for a new dress and she was really sad because she couldn't afford it. She even cried. But then I said I didn't want it and it was ok."

Tanya was upset the entire day. She came home and her mother noticed she was very quiet. She asked Tanya the reason for her sadness. Tanya explained everything to her mother. She became upset, too. Rita's mother was her old friend. She felt sorry for her and her daughter..

"Mom, it is not fair! Rita and her mom will not get anything for Dhanteras!" "Yes, my dear. It is unfair. That is why I and your father always say you should be grateful for everything you get. There are kids your age who don't get the things you get every day. You should always know that you are blessed and think before you demand."

On Sunday, they go to the bicycle shop to get Tanya her fancy bicycle. She got the one with glitter paint and was very happy. Then they go to the mall to get Tanya her Aladdin bag and her magic pen. They got the magic pen and extra ink refills with it. When Tanya was told to select a bag, she chose a pink Barbie bag. Her mother was a bit surprised. She asked, "Didn't you want the Aladdin one?" "Yes mom, but now I want this one."

The next day she didn't use her new bag for school. She used her old bag. Her mother asked why didn't use the new one. After all, she wanted that new bag.

"Yes, mom but I thought Rita needs a new bag more than I. She loves Barbie and so instead of getting myself a new bag, I got her a new one. After all, isn't Diwali about making people happy?"

Her mother said, "Yes, dear. That is a good idea but you could've asked for two bags - one for yourself and one for Rita. Then you could both have new bags."

"Yes, mom. But that day Rita told me that parents work hard for us kids. I didn't want to demand more. And you and dad have already given me a new bike! I will ride to school on that."

Her mother was very proud of her little daughter and kissed her. She said, "You are growing too fast, O child."

"Mom, can we invite Rita and her mother to our house for the remaining days of Diwali. She will love to celebrate with us!"

"Of course, Tanya! Happiness multiplies when you share it with others! It would be great to spend time with them, I haven't seen Rita's mom for a long time."

Rita was very happy to get a new bag and she hugged Tanya. They both celebrated the remaining four days of Diwali together.

Thank you for choosing *5-minute Diwali Stories for Kids*.
We hope you spent a lovely time with it!
We put a whole heart into preparing this book
so we would appreciate your opinion on Amazon.

If you want to receive
information about new books
or you have any suggestions for our future publications please contact us:
es.publishing.amazon@gmail.com.

Happy Diwali!

Made in the USA
Las Vegas, NV
28 October 2024

10649914R00044